IMMIGRANTS
WHO SERVED THE NATION

BY ERIC BRAUN

CAPSTONE PRESS
a capstone imprint

Capstone Captivate is published by Capstone Press, an imprint of Capstone.
1710 Roe Crest Drive
North Mankato, Minnesota 56003
www.capstonepub.com

Library of Congress Cataloging-in-Publication Data is available
on the Library of Congress website.

ISBN: 978-1-4966-9596-3 (library binding)
ISBN: 978-1-4966-9680-9 (paperback)
ISBN: 978-1-9771-5444-6 (eBook pdf)

Summary: Some of the most important roles in American life have been filled by
people born outside the United States. Immigrants have served in the military
since before the Civil War. Some immigrants have made fortunes and given them
away—to create libraries, fund after-school programs, and protect citizens' civil
rights. Still others have held political office or served our nation as ambassadors
or—literally—rocket scientists. Here are 25 immigrants who have served our nation
in these and other important ways.

Image Credits

Alamy: AB Forces News Collection, 17, Moviestore Collection Ltd, 47; Associated
Press: Toby Talbot, 32; Courtesy of Kashoua Kristy Yang, Photo by Lacy Landre: 5
(bottom left), 35; Getty Images: AFP/Robyn Beck, 14, Bettmann, 9, 28, Bloomberg/
Andrew Harrer, 23, Hulton Archive, 30, Space Frontiers, 46; Library of Congress: 5
(top left, middle right), 7, 19; NASA: cover, 1, 5 (background, middle left), 25, 44, 56;
Newscom: CQ Roll Call/Tom Williams, 37, Reuters/Mike Segar, 58, Reuters/William
Philpott, 52, SIPA/AdMedia/CNP/Alex Edelman, 42, UPI Photo Service/Roger L.
Wollenberg, 54, ZUMA Press/Bryan Smith, 11, ZUMA Press/Keystone Pictures
USA, 50; Shutterstock: Alexandros Michailidis, 27, dennizn, 22, Featureflash Photo
Agency, 33, My Hardy (background texture), 22, 28, 47, S-F, 21; U.S. Department of
State: 48; U.S. Marine Corps: 5 (top right), 12, Sgt. Gabriela Garcia, 13; Wikimedia:
U.S. House Office of Photography/Kristie Boyd, 5 (bottom right), 39

Editorial Credits

Editor: Michelle Bisson; Designers: Kayla Rossow and Tracy Davies;
Media Researcher: Svetlana Zhurkin; Production Specialist: Tori Abraham

All internet sites appearing in back matter were available and accurate when this
book was sent to press.

TABLE OF CONTENTS

INTRODUCTION

In order for a democracy to work, many people must contribute their time, knowledge, and expertise. For a democracy to *thrive*, those people must come from all walks of life. They need to represent all citizens. In the United States, immigrants have served in a wide range of roles. They have helped make laws more fair and helpful to all. They have fought for peace and justice and stood up for what they believed was right. They have given their ideas as well as their wealth to improve the lives of others. In some cases, they have even given their lives.

Those who have come to the United States to serve have done it for many reasons. Some were fleeing war or oppression. Some sought more freedom or a better opportunity than they could get in their home countries. Some were simply looking for a different life. They came for many reasons, but they stayed because by serving their new country, they could make it better.

Franz Sigel

Rafael Peralta

Andrew Carnegie

Anousheh Ansari

Kashoua Kristy Yang

Ilhan Omar

CHAPTER ONE

PROTECTING THEIR COUNTRY

People can serve their nation in many ways. One of the bravest is to join the military and risk their very lives. These immigrants chose to protect their country from harm, no matter the cost.

FRANZ SIGEL

(1824–1902)
Born in Sinsheim, Germany

Franz Sigel was born in a small town in southwest Baden (now Germany). He served as a lieutenant in the Baden army. He later joined the revolution against the German Confederation. Sigel became an important leader. But he fled Germany in 1849.

Sigel immigrated to New York City in 1852. He worked as a teacher, musician, surveyor, and magazine publisher. He also owned a store. By February 1861, he'd moved to St. Louis, Missouri. There he joined the Union Army to fight in the Civil War (1861–1865).

He was appointed second lieutenant and then colonel. He served under General Nathaniel Lyon.

By this time, Sigel had become popular among German Americans. He was especially effective at getting them to join the Union cause.

Sigel's greatest victory came in March 1862. It was at the Battle of Pea Ridge in

Franz Sigel's leadership and bravery inspired other German Americans to fight for the Union.

northwest Arkansas. His troops defeated the army of Confederate major general Earl Van Dorn. Sigel was then promoted to major general. General "Stonewall" Jackson later defeated him at the Second Battle of Bull Run. But Sigel was praised for his efforts against the larger army.

Sigel died August 21, 1902. More than 25,000 people attended his visitation. Many of them were German Americans. Schools, parks, and ships were named after him. Statues were erected in St. Louis and New York.

DID YOU KNOW?

Immigrants made up about 13 percent of the U.S. population during the Civil War. About one out of every four members of the Union Army was born overseas.

CHIEN-SHIUNG WU

(1912–1997)
Born in Jiangsu province, China

Chien-Shiung Wu grew up to be a scientist. She did groundbreaking work in nuclear physics. But that never would have happened if not for her parents. They believed that girls deserved to be educated. That was almost unheard of in their small town in eastern China.

Wu was a gifted student. In 1936, she came to the United States to continue her education. She was 24.

Chien-Shiung Wu in her lab at Columbia University in New York City in 1963

Wu studied physics in Berkeley, California. The next year, Japan invaded China, and soon thereafter World War II (1939–1945) broke out in Asia. Wu lost contact with her family.

Wu continued her research while teaching at Smith College in Massachusetts. Later she taught at Princeton University in New Jersey. Wu was looking at beta decay. This is a process that occurs inside the nucleus of an atom. She faced great sexism and racism. Still, she was recruited to be a part of the Manhattan Project. Its job was to build the world's first atomic bomb during World War II.

Wu's greatest accomplishment came after the war. She created a way to test a physics law known as "conservation of parity." Her experiments disproved the law. The men on her team won the Nobel Prize for the discovery in 1957. But as the only woman on the team, Wu received no credit. Later in her life she campaigned hard for women's equality in science.

FANG WONG

(1948–)
Born in Guangzhou, China

The American Legion is a service organization for veterans of the American military. It has long fought for recognition and better benefits for those who have served. When Fang Wong was elected the Legion's national commander in 2011, he did not change its goals. But he brought new focus to certain issues. A big one was how long veterans had to wait to receive benefits from the Veterans Administration (VA). Many veterans had to wait years for the VA to process claims. Those claims would help them with health care or disabilities.

Wong immigrated to the United States from China in 1960. He was 12. When the United States entered

In 2011, Fang Wong became the first Asian American to be elected the National Commander of the American Legion.

the Vietnam War (1955–1975), he enlisted in the U.S. Army. He served 25 months in Vietnam, earning a Bronze Star for heroic service in combat. He retired in 1989 with the rank of chief warrant officer 3.

As the American Legion's leader, Wong lobbied the VA from the outside. In 2016, he was appointed to the Advisory Committee on Minority Veterans. This 12-member panel is part of the VA. The panel briefs the U.S. Congress and the VA secretary. It tells them how the department is administering benefits and services to the country's 4.9 million veterans of color.

Wong's goal has always been to make life better for those who have served their country in the military.

RAFAEL PERALTA

(1979–2004)
Born in Mexico City, Mexico

In November 2004, 25-year-old Marine Sergeant Rafael Peralta volunteered to lead a dangerous mission. His team of eight men had to clear insurgents out of several buildings in Fallujah, Iraq. In one building, they found the first two rooms empty. But then Peralta led his men into the third room. A spray of machine gunfire hit him.

Rafael Peralta gave his life to save his fellow soldiers while serving in Iraq in 2004.

Peralta fell to the floor. Suddenly, a yellow grenade bounced in from a connecting room.

Peralta pulled the grenade under his body. When it blew, it killed him instantly. But by smothering the grenade, he shielded the other men from the explosion.

In October 2015, members of the armed forces attended the dedication ceremony for the Navy destroyer USS *Rafael Peralta*.

Peralta immigrated to the United States from Mexico at age 15. His mother said he wanted to be a Marine from the day he moved to San Diego, California. He signed up as soon as he became a permanent resident.

For saving his fellow soldiers, Peralta was awarded the Navy Cross. That's the second-highest honor a Marine can get. In October 2015, the Navy named a new destroyer the USS *Rafael Peralta*.

YEA JI SEA

(1989–)
Born in South Korea

In 2008, the U.S. government started a program called Military Accessions Vital to the National Interest (MAVNI). This program allowed noncitizens in the United States to enlist if they had critical skills the military needed. After serving, they could apply for U.S. citizenship.

Through MAVNI, Yea Ji Sea joined the U.S. Army in 2013. She dreamed of becoming a citizen. She was born in South Korea and arrived in the United States when she was nine. She had two critical skills. One was that she spoke fluent Korean. The other was that she qualified as a health-care specialist.

Yea Ji Sea talks to the press after becoming a U.S. citizen in 2018.

Sea served the United States in South Korea in many ways. She was an ambulance aid driver and a pharmacy technician. She served as a translator for doctors. She helped care for injured soldiers. Sea earned two Army Achievement Medals "for exceptionally meritorious service."

But when she finished her service, there was a problem. She had unknowingly worked with a corrupt language school when she was younger. The school had worked illegally to get some students citizenship. This made her application for citizenship look suspicious. Instead of becoming a citizen, she could have been deported. Thankfully, the American Civil Liberties Union took her case to court. A judge ruled in her favor. On August 24, 2018, Sea was sworn in as a U.S. citizen.

DID YOU KNOW?

Even before the MAVNI program, the United States had a long history of immigrants serving in the military as part of a path to legal citizenship. During World War II, at least 100,000 noncitizens served. About 31,000 soldiers born outside the country became U.S. citizens by serving in the Korean War (1950–1953).

MARIA DAUME

(c. 1998–)
Born in Russia

Maria Daume's path to becoming a U.S. Marine was tougher than most. She and her twin brother, Nikolai, were born in a Russian prison in Siberia. They lived there with their mother until she died. Then they were moved to an orphanage. When they were 4 years old, an American couple adopted the pair. In high school in New York, Daume was bullied for being Russian. She was also bullied for having a birth parent who died in prison.

Daume had something else working against her: She was a woman. She wanted to fight—not work some desk job. "I think everything about it is for me," she said about combat. "And I want to prove that females can do it."

Combat jobs in the military had only recently opened up to women. It was a controversial idea. Many people were against it. But Daume completed "the Crucible," the extremely intense infantry training. Doing so showed that women were capable of being Marines.

Maria Daume (left) receives the Eagle, Globe, and Anchor emblem from her drill instructor after successfully completing "the Crucible" training.

Daume finished the training on March 23, 2017. With that, she was among the first women to serve in the U.S. Marines infantry.

CHAPTER TWO

GIVING BACK TO OTHERS

Many people dream of striking it rich. For those who achieve that dream, the desire to give back to the society that lifted them up can be strong. From giants of industry to titans of technology, these immigrants gave their fortunes to make their nation, and the world, a better place.

ANDREW CARNEGIE

(1835–1919)
Born in Dunfermline, Scotland

Andrew Carnegie was born in Scotland in 1835. He received little formal education. But his belief in the value of education formed the core of his giving.

When Carnegie was 13, his family moved to Allegheny, Pennsylvania. There, he went to work in a factory. He later worked as a telegraph operator. In 1853, Carnegie became the assistant to one of the most important officials with the Pennsylvania Railroad. In that position, he learned about business. He was soon promoted to superintendent.

Andrew Carnegie funded thousands of libraries and colleges across the United States to help improve people's lives through education.

Carnegie began investing money in other companies. After the Civil War, he founded the Keystone Bridge Company. The company replaced wooden bridges with stronger steel ones. His Carnegie Steel Company transformed the way steel was made. Carnegie was a shrewd businessman. By 1868, he was worth $400,000 (nearly $5 million today).

Just after the turn of the century, Carnegie made a big change. He sold his business for more than $480 million (more than $14.5 billion today). He spent the rest of his life helping others. He believed strongly in the value of education. He donated $5 million to the New York Public Library so it could open more branches.

Carnegie also supported the opening of more than 2,800 other libraries. In 1900, he donated $1 million to create the Carnegie Technical Schools. This school for working-class men and women later merged with the Mellon Institute to become Carnegie Mellon University. In 1910, he formed the Carnegie Endowment for International Peace. This think tank is dedicated to advancing world peace.

CYRUS TANG

(1930–2018)
Born in Suzhou, China

The Chinese revolution turned China to communism in 1949. The new government took ownership of most privately owned real estate. This included what was owned by Cyrus Tang's family. In 1950, at age 20, Tang came to the United States to go to school.

Tang settled in Chicago, Illinois. There, he tried to launch a Chinese restaurant business. But it failed. He then took a job in a steel plant. He began working his way up. To earn extra money, he imported and sold straw hats from China. In 1964, he had saved enough money to start his own steel warehouse business.

The Cyrus Tang Foundation has funded the Field Museum in Chicago. The museum features the Cyrus Tang Hall of China, a permanent exhibition that teaches visitors about China.

Over time, Tang expanded that business. He also became involved in many others. He became a billionaire. But Tang's goal was always about more than making money. "I believe success in life is not based on assets gained or knowledge acquired," he said. "It is how we make use of what we have to contribute to society."

Tang's giving focused on the areas of public policy, community development, education, and health care. Tang supported nonpartisan voter education. He also funded research into hospitals and traditional medicine. This kind of medicine means medical skills and practices used by indigenous cultures. He awarded more than 100,000 scholarships to students in grades 8 through college. He was known to many of these students as "Grandpa." He built schools in rural areas. Tang regularly gave gifts of tens of millions of dollars to many foundations.

PIERRE OMIDYAR

(1967–)
Born in Paris, France

Pierre Omidyar was born in Paris to Iranian parents. His family moved to Maryland for his father's work. Omidyar was interested in computers from an early age. He wrote his first computer program when he was 14. The program cataloged books for his school library.

Omidyar graduated college with a computer science degree in 1988. Then he worked in software

Pierre Omidyar used part of the fortune he made from eBay to fund nonprofits.

development. He helped start a company called Ink Development Corporation in 1991.

Life changed for Omidyar during the summer of 1995. He created a page on his website where people could list items to sell by auction. The page was extremely popular and grew rapidly. He renamed it eBay. He charged a small fee to let people sell their items on it. Soon, eBay's profits exploded, making Omidyar wealthy.

In 1998, Omidyar and his wife cofounded the Omidyar Foundation to support nonprofits. He expanded it into the Omidyar Network in 2004. Through his network, he has given more than $1 billion to programs and causes. His gifts have focused on reducing poverty. He has also given to aid human rights and disaster relief.

One part of the network is an organization called Luminate. Luminate hopes to stem the rise of authoritarianism and increasing social divisions. It gives grants and investments that help people engage in government. Luminate also helps people protect their data and digital rights. It promotes investigative journalism and aids those trying to create a more just and informed society.

ANOUSHEH ANSARI

(1966–)
Born in Mashhad, Iran

On September 18, 2006, Anousheh Ansari went into space. But she was not part of a government program. That made her the world's fourth private industry space explorer. And it made her the first female private space explorer. She was also the first astronaut of Iranian descent.

Anousheh Ansari holds a plant grown in space during her stay on the International Space Station.

Ansari grew up in Tehran, Iran. She moved to the United States in 1984. She did not speak English when she arrived. Still, she earned a bachelor's degree in electronics and computer engineering and later a master's degree in electrical engineering. In 1993, she teamed up with her husband and brother-in-law. They founded Telecom Technologies, Inc., a telecommunications company.

Ansari had long been interested in space flight. Her business had made her wealthy. So she and her brother-in-law made a multimillion-dollar contribution to the XPRIZE Foundation. This nonprofit organization runs competitions to encourage innovations that help people.

With Ansari's gift, the foundation established the Ansari XPRIZE. This was a cash award of $10 million. It went to the first private company to launch a reusable manned spacecraft into space twice within two weeks. After an aerospace company won the prize, Ansari arranged to participate in a space flight.

Ansari has supported several nonprofit organizations. These include the Make-a-Wish Foundation. Another is the Iranian American Women Foundation. She has also supported the Ashoka organization, which supports social entrepreneurs. Those are organizations with the goal of making social change.

GEORGE SOROS

(1930–)
Born in Budapest, Hungary

György Schwartz was 6 years old in 1936, when he and his family changed their last name to Soros. They did this because anti-Semitism was growing in Hungary, where they lived. They felt safer if their name didn't give them away as Jewish people. Soros was 13 when the Nazis invaded Hungary in March 1944.

By 2018, George Soros had donated more than $32 billion to his philanthropic organization, the Open Society Foundations.

The Soros family survived World War II by posing as Christians, and they helped others do so too.

After the war, Soros moved to England to study economics. There he became interested in the writings of the philosopher Karl Popper. Popper believed that societies can only succeed when people's individual rights are respected.

In 1956, Soros moved to New York. There he began his career in finance. He began to build his fortune. Within decades, he was one of the richest people in the world.

In 1979, Soros started giving money away to help others. His causes have typically been guided by the lessons he learned about respect for individual rights.

His organization, Open Society Foundations, gives aid to regions struck by natural disaster. It establishes after-school programs. It funds the arts and fights disease. Soros has also supported causes that advance justice, public health, and independent media.

IMMIGRATION DURING WORLD WAR II

Anti-Semitism influenced U.S. immigration policy during World War II. The government restricted immigration from Europe. About 125,000 Germans came to the United States between 1933 and 1945. Most of them were Jewish. But that was only about 10 percent of the quota allowed by law. That means the United States could have saved 10 times more Jewish people from Nazi persecution in Germany alone.

A group of children fleeing Nazi Germany in 1939 look on as their ship passes the Statue of Liberty in New York Harbor.

CHAPTER THREE

SERVING IN OFFICE

Every nation has a government. But in order for that government to work, it needs people who are willing to lead. These immigrants chose to serve in office to help lead their nation and shape its laws.

JOSEPH PULITZER

(1847–1911)
Born in Makó, Hungary

Born in Hungary, Joseph Pulitzer moved to Germany when he was 17. He hoped to join a European army to make a living. Instead, American military recruiters persuaded him to come to the United States. He joined the North in the Civil War.

After the war, he worked and studied English at a library in St. Louis, Missouri. There he befriended the editors of a German-language newspaper. Pulitzer was fluent in German. They offered him a job as a reporter.

Pulitzer became active in the Republican Party. He won election to the Missouri state legislature and took

Joseph Pulitzer's will gave Columbia University $2 million to establish a graduate journalism school and create the Pulitzer Prizes.

office in January 1870. In 1872, he joined the Liberal Republican Party. But that party soon collapsed. He then switched to the Democratic Party. In 1876, Pulitzer campaigned for Democratic presidential candidate Samuel J. Tilden.

Meanwhile, Pulitzer had become an excellent journalist. He bought the German-language paper. Later he bought the *St. Louis Post-Dispatch*. Pulitzer grew wealthy. And his political ambitions rose. He was elected to the U.S. House of Representatives in 1884.

Pulitzer made an important mark on American society. He raised money to build a stone pedestal for the Statue of Liberty in New York Harbor. After his death, his fortune was used to establish the Pulitzer Prizes. The prizes reward excellence in American journalism, photography, literature, history, poetry, music, and drama.

DID YOU KNOW?

The number and categories of Pulitzer Prizes have varied over the years. Currently, 14 prizes in journalism, 6 prizes in letters, and 1 prize in music are awarded each year.

MADELEINE MAY KUNIN

(1933–)
Born in Zürich, Switzerland

Only one woman has ever been elected to three terms as governor of a state. That woman is Madeleine May Kunin.

Kunin was born in Zürich, Switzerland. Her father died before she was 3 years old. As the Nazis gained power in Europe, her mother moved the family, which was Jewish, several times to keep them safe.

Madeleine May Kunin takes the oath of office to become the first woman governor of Vermont on January 10, 1985.

In 1940, the family fled to the United States. Though Kunin's immediate family was now safe, several of her relatives died in the Holocaust. She later said that this tragedy had a big impact on her identity. "This was the source of my political courage," she said. "I could do what the victims could not: oppose evil whenever I recognized it."

Though Kunin faced discrimination because she was a woman, she started a career as a journalist at the *Burlington Free Press*. In 1972, she ran for and was elected to the Vermont House of Representatives. She was reelected twice, then served two terms as lieutenant governor.

In 1984, Kunin ran for governor of Vermont. She won and was reelected twice. In her years as governor, Kunin promoted feminism and made a point of hiring many women for positions on her staff and roles in the executive and judicial branches.

Kunin later served as the U.S. deputy secretary of education and as U.S. ambassador to Switzerland. As ambassador, she helped create a compensation fund for Holocaust survivors.

ARNOLD SCHWARZENEGGER

(1947–)
Born in Thal, Austria

As a boy, Arnold Schwarzenegger's father made fun of him. Why? Schwarzenegger dreamed of becoming a famous bodybuilder. Still, he worked hard to achieve his goal. He exercised in his basement and later at gyms.

But Schwarzenegger also dreamed of going to the

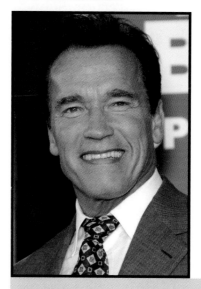

Arnold Schwarzenegger served as California's governor from 2003 to 2011 before returning to his career as an actor.

United States. In 1965, at age 18, his dreams started to become real. He began winning bodybuilding competitions. At age 21, he moved to America.

Schwarzenegger had confidence and a sense of humor to go with his powerful body. He soon caught the eye of movie producers. He starred in many movies. But by the 1990s, Schwarzenegger began to set his sights on politics. He became a public activist for the Republican Party. In 2003, he ran for governor of California and won.

As governor, Schwarzenegger did much to improve the state's finances. He also helped to promote new businesses and protect the environment. One of his greatest achievements was the Global Warming Solutions Act of 2006. This bipartisan agreement helped combat global warming by reducing California's greenhouse gas emissions.

He traveled the country and the world promoting California-grown products and technologies. Health and fitness had always been important to him. He signed laws making the state's school nutrition standards the most progressive in the nation.

KASHOUA KRISTY YANG

(1980–)
Born in Thailand

Kashoua Kristy Yang was born in a refugee camp in Thailand. Growing up, she heard wonderful stories about America. Her family moved to the United States when she was 6 years old. They settled in Wisconsin, and Yang quickly learned English and soaked up U.S. culture.

Yang eventually earned a computer science degree. Then something happened to change her path. Her brother was badly injured after being struck by a car.

In 2019, Kashoua Kristy Yang received the Forward Under 40 Award from the University of Wisconsin Alumni Association for the achievements she has made before turning 40 years old.

It was challenging for him and the family to get through the confusing health-care and legal systems. For those with financial or language barriers, it can be difficult to get justice. So Yang went to law school.

When Yang became a lawyer, her goal was to help others. She worked with people on many issues. These included family law, workplace injury, and disability lawsuits. Then she realized she could do more to help others as a judge. In 2017, she ran to be a Milwaukee County circuit court judge. When she won, she became the second Hmong American judge in the United States. She was also the first female Hmong judge and the first elected, without appointment, in the country. Each day she works to clear the path to justice for all.

MAZIE HIRONO

(1947–)
Born in Fukushima, Japan

U.S. Senator Mazie Hirono of Hawaii is polite, quiet, and calm. But don't let that fool you. She has been a fighter her whole life.

Hirono learned how to fight from her mother. Her father was an alcoholic. He stole from the family

Mazie Hirono was the first Asian American woman to win a seat in the U.S. Senate.

to pay for his gambling habit. Her mother hatched a secret plan to escape. She and her children moved to Hawaii to start over. There, she worked two minimum-wage jobs to support her son and daughter.

Hirono successfully ran for a seat in the Hawaii House of Representatives in 1980. She became chair of the House Consumer Protection and Commerce Committee. There, she focused on greater protections for Hawaii's workers and consumers.

In 1994, Hirono was elected lieutenant governor. Again, she focused on fighting for ordinary people.

She was a leader in revamping Hawaii's workers' compensation insurance laws. She also improved early childhood education. Hirono was elected to the U.S. House of Representatives in 2006 and to the U.S. Senate in 2012. She is the Senate's only immigrant and its first female Asian American.

Hirono is a member of the Senate Armed Services and Veterans Affairs committees. She works to help service members, veterans, and their families. Hirono has written bills to promote clean energy use by the military and invest in the education, training, and treatment of service members. She fights against efforts to take away health care and weaken civil rights.

ILHAN OMAR

(1982–)
Born in Mogadishu, Somalia

Just before the presidential election in November 2016, candidate Donald Trump held a campaign rally in Minnesota. He spoke about his opposition to immigration. He called out immigrants from Somalia. Many Somali live in Minnesota. He called them "terror prone." He promised to prevent more from coming to the United States.

As a U.S. representative, Ilhan Omar has served on the House Budget Committee, the House Foreign Affairs Committee, and the House Committee on Education and Labor.

Three days later, Trump won the presidency. And Ilhan Omar won election to the Minnesota House of Representatives. She was the first-ever Somali state lawmaker in the nation.

Omar and her family fled civil war in Somalia when she was 8 years old. They eventually settled in a neighborhood of Minneapolis with a large Somali community. She soon became interested in politics.

Many young activists and community members felt ignored by the government. Omar began to make connections with these groups. She inspired them.

When she won her state seat, voter turnout in her district increased by 37 percent. Two years later, she successfully ran for a U.S. House seat.

As a U.S. representative, Omar has gained a high profile. Not only has she cosponsored hundreds of bills but she has also criticized the president for his anti-immigrant policies and language. Her bold approach has attracted criticism and even death threats. But many others, especially immigrants, find hope in her focus on civil rights and human rights.

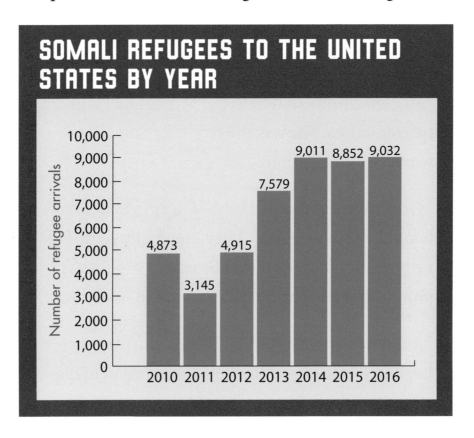

SOMALI REFUGEES TO THE UNITED STATES BY YEAR

PRAMILA JAYAPAL

(1965–)
Born in Chennai, India

Pramila Jayapal joined the U.S. Congress in 2016. Since then, she has fought for important progressive causes. These include health care for all and a bold plan to fight global warming. They also include smarter, more humane immigration policies. As these ideas have gained popularity nationwide, she has become a prominent voice in the Democratic Party. She is able to champion activist ideas as a political insider.

Jayapal was born in India. She came to the United States alone when she was 16 to go to college. She earned bachelor's and master's degrees. She worked in many different industries. She also became an activist for issues such as public health, women's rights, civil rights, and immigrants' rights. Yet, she often lived in fear of losing her chance at citizenship. "For years, I had this deep worry that I was not going to be let into this country, which had become my home, but I wasn't a citizen," Jayapal said.

Pramila Jayapal speaks at a U.S. House Judiciary Committee hearing in December 2019.

Jayapal knows that thousands of immigrants live with that fear every day as anti-immigration laws have gotten stricter. As a U.S. congresswoman representing Washington State, her goal is to change immigration laws. She wants to make sure families are not separated at the border. She wants to ensure that immigrants can get work visas that match their skills. Because of her fast rise in politics, Jayapal is well positioned to help make that happen.

CHAPTER FOUR

ANSWERING THE CALL

Many people have a calling in life. For some it's a special skill they have or a talent they've shaped. For others, it's a cause they believe in. No matter the calling, these immigrants followed their passions and served their nation along the way.

WERNHER VON BRAUN

(1912–1977)
Born in Wyrzysk, Poland

Wernher von Braun was the director of the U.S. National Aeronautics and Space Administration's (NASA's) Marshall Space Flight Center from 1960 to 1970. In that role, he oversaw some of the country's biggest space accomplishments. Perhaps the biggest was the Saturn V rocket for the Apollo 8 spacecraft. Apollo 8 orbited the moon in 1968.

But von Braun didn't grow up dreaming of being an American space leader. He was born to wealthy parents in Wyrzysk, Germany (now part of Poland).

Wernher von Braun stands in front of a Saturn V rocket being prepared for the Apollo 11 mission to the moon in 1969.

Von Braun loved astronomy. He earned a doctorate in physics from the University of Berlin. He went on to work in missile development. He was part of the group that built the supersonic antiaircraft missile known as the V-2 or "Vengeance Weapon 2."

In 1937, von Braun joined the Nazi Party. Three years later he joined the SS, a notorious Nazi guard unit. But history is unclear on his loyalty to the Nazi Party. He was briefly sent to prison by Nazi Germany's secret police.

By 1945, von Braun was out of prison. He turned himself over to U.S. troops and was flown to the United States. There he worked with the army's guided missile project. He became a U.S. citizen in 1955. After his work with NASA in the 1960s, von Braun remained active in the aerospace industry until his death in Virginia in 1977.

As someone who built rockets both for the Nazis and for the United States, his legacy is complicated. But his contributions to space travel were groundbreaking.

FAROUK EL-BAZ

(1938–)
Born in El-Senbellawein, Egypt

In 1969, NASA was planning the Apollo 11 mission. The mission would land the first humans on the moon. Scientists had to research many complex issues. One of them was exactly where on the moon they should land. To decide, they turned to a scientist named Farouk El-Baz.

El-Baz was an expert in geology. He studied the various rocks and other terrain of the moon. He studied photographs of the moon's surface.

Farouk El-Baz (right) briefs astronauts Ronald Evans (center) and Robert Overmyer on lunar geology prior to the Apollo 17 lunar landing mission in 1972.

And he identified the safest spot for a lunar landing. Then El-Baz trained the astronauts on how to observe and record the geology of the moon.

El-Baz grew up in Egypt. In 1960, he moved to the United States to attend graduate school. He earned a doctorate in geology. Later, he was tapped to work with NASA. After the successful moon landing, he continued working on the Apollo program. He played a key role in the Apollo 15 rover mission in 1971. The astronauts said he was a terrific teacher.

The Apollo program ended in 1972. By then, El-Baz had secured his place as one of the world's leading geologists. He is currently a leading expert in the study of deserts and water using space images.

CULTURAL ICON

Farouk El-Baz has become a cultural icon. One episode of *Star Trek: The Next Generation* had a spacecraft named El-Baz. In 1998, Tom Hanks developed a TV series about the Apollo moon landing. One segment was titled "The Brain of Farouk El-Baz."

Commander Will Riker (left) and Worf, played by actors Jonathan Frakes and Michael Dorn, stand next to the El-Baz spacecraft.

HENRY KISSINGER

(1923–)
Born in Fürth, Germany

Henry Kissinger was 15 years old when he and his family fled Nazi Germany in 1938. They wanted to escape the discrimination and possible death they faced as Jewish people. Five years later, Kissinger was back in Germany. This time he was fighting the Nazis as a U.S. Army soldier and intelligence officer.

Henry Kissinger was the first immigrant to the United States to receive the Nobel Peace Prize.

Kissinger's family had arrived—poor—in New York City. Kissinger worked in a factory and learned English. He graduated from high school. He began college and became a U.S. citizen. At the end of World War II, he returned to college at Harvard University. He went on to earn a doctorate in government studies and become a professor.

Kissinger was teaching at Harvard in 1969 when President Lyndon Johnson asked him to serve as the country's national security advisor. The United States was in the middle of the controversial Vietnam War. Many Americans viewed the war as a fight between democracy and communism. But others viewed it as an unnecessary war that caused the deaths of innocent people.

For four years, Kissinger oversaw the U.S. role in the Vietnam War. In 1973, he signed a peace treaty with the North Vietnamese government. He received the Nobel Peace Prize for ending U.S. involvement in the war.

Again, there was controversy. Some thought Kissinger was a brilliant statesman who had achieved peace. Others thought he had kept the war going for four unnecessary years, causing thousands of deaths.

Nearly everyone agrees that Kissinger was one of the most influential diplomats in U.S. history.

Henry Kissinger shakes hands with Xuan Thuy, Chief of the North Vietnamese delegation, during peace negotiations in 1973.

MADELEINE ALBRIGHT

(1937–)
Born in Prague, the Czech Republic

In 1999, U.S. Secretary of State Madeleine Albright made a tough decision. She called for bombing the Kosovo region of Yugoslavia. The region was in the midst of the Kosovo War (1998–1999), and Yugoslavian forces had been killing its Albanian citizens for their ethnicity. Albright believed that military force was the only way to stop this humanitarian crisis.

Many Americans disagreed with her plan. They called it an unnecessary use of force. But joint NATO forces went on to bomb the area for 11 weeks. Finally, the Yugoslavian military agreed to end its ethnic cleansing campaign. It was a great victory for Albright.

Albright's ties to the region were strong. She was born just a few hundred miles from Kosovo, in Prague. At that time, the city was the capital of Czechoslovakia. She was 2 years old when the Nazis invaded that nation. Her family fled to England. They returned to Prague after World War II, but they immigrated to the United States in 1948.

U.S. Secretary of State Madeleine Albright takes questions from reporters during a press conference in 1999.

Albright became a professor of International Relations at Georgetown University in Washington, D.C. In 1993, President Bill Clinton named her ambassador to the United Nations. In that role, she spent four years arguing for more military interventions around the world to fight oppression and expand human rights.

In December 1996, President Clinton nominated her to be secretary of state. When she was sworn in, she became the first woman to hold that position.

ELAINE CHAO

(1953–)
Born in Taipei, Taiwan

Elaine Chao was sworn in on January 29, 2001, as U.S. secretary of labor. That made her the first Asian American woman to become a cabinet secretary in the U.S. government. As labor secretary, she was responsible for setting policy for workers and businesses across the nation.

Chao was born in Taiwan to Chinese parents. Her father came to the United States on a scholarship in 1958. Three years later, Chao and her mother and two younger sisters joined him. They spent 37 days on a freight ship making the journey. Elaine was 8. Chao later said of her mother, "She and my father are part of a generation that experienced much suffering, but achieved great things."

Chao graduated from Mount Holyoke College and the Harvard Business School. Then she began a career in the banking industry. During the 1980s and 1990s, she served in both government and nonprofit leadership roles. She was director of the Peace Corps.

Elaine Chao stands with President George W. Bush after being named as his choice for secretary of labor in 2001.

Chao was also president and CEO of the United Way of America, a charitable organization.

President George W. Bush appointed her to head the Department of Labor. She became the longest-serving secretary of labor since Frances Perkins served from 1933 to 1945 under President Franklin D. Roosevelt. In 2017, Chao again became a cabinet secretary. President Trump appointed her to lead the Department of Transportation.

AVE KLUDZE

(1966–)
Born in Hohoe, Ghana

As a boy, Ave Kludze was very curious. In fact, he was so curious, his parents didn't like to leave him home alone because they knew he'd take apart the radio.

Why would he do that? It was the only way to find out how it worked.

Kludze grew up in the Volta region of Ghana. He came to the United States in the late 1980s. He earned his bachelor's degree at Rutgers University in New Jersey. Kludze had planned to return to Ghana. He wanted to work on building up solar energy resources for his country. Instead, he found a job at NASA. He helps develop and fly spacecraft.

Kludze has worked on many NASA projects. In 2003, the space shuttle Columbia exploded while reentering the atmosphere. After that disaster, Kludze was selected to join the NASA Engineering and Safety Center (NESC) as a systems expert. In 2004, he and a group of engineers designed the

Extravehicular Activity Infrared (EVA IR) camera for space-walking astronauts. The EVA IR is critical for safety inspections. In 2006, the Calipso environmental satellite was launched. Kludze served as a systems engineer for it.

Kludze's curiosity has carried him a long way. He hopes more young Africans will follow him on that journey by becoming scientists.

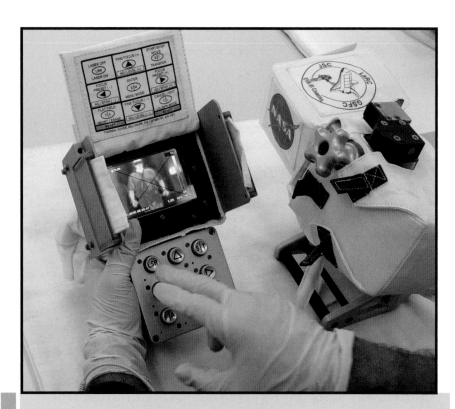

Ave Kludze helped design the EVA IR camera, shown here in a NASA lab, to detect damage on the exterior of a space shuttle.

PREET BHARARA

(1968–)
Born in Firozpur, India

Preet Bharara was born in Firozpur, India. He was a toddler when he moved to New Jersey with his family in 1970. He later got a law degree from Columbia Law School in New York. He was an assistant U.S. attorney in Manhattan for five years before becoming a U.S. attorney.

In August 2009, Bharara took over as the leader of one of the most important law enforcement agencies in the United States. President Barack Obama appointed him U.S. attorney for the Southern District of New York.

Preet Bharara poses with *Doing Justice*, a best-selling book he wrote about his time in government.

Bharara fearlessly prosecuted powerful gang leaders and mafia bosses. He also tried billionaire hedge-fund swindlers. He went after international terrorists, arms dealers, and more. He prosecuted corrupt politicians, both Democrats and Republicans. He loved his job and was proud of his office's work.

When Donald Trump won the presidential election in 2016, he invited Bharara to a meeting. He let Bharara know that he wanted him to stay on in his position. But within months, it became known that Bharara's office was investigating Trump's lawyer and his lawyer's organization. Upon learning that, the president fired him.

Since his firing, Bharara has become a vocal critic of Trump. He has a big platform. In 2020, he had nearly 1.3 million Twitter followers. His podcast, *Stay Tuned*, is hugely popular. It discusses the link between politics and law. His first book, *Doing Justice*, released in 2019, was a best seller.

TIMELINE

1862 Franz Sigel defeats Confederate major general Earl Van Dorn at the Battle of Pea Ridge during the Civil War.

1884 Wealthy newspaper publisher Joseph Pulitzer is elected to the U.S. House of Representatives.

1910 Andrew Carnegie forms the Carnegie Endowment for International Peace, a think tank dedicated to advancing world peace.

1957 Chien-Shiung Wu's male colleagues win the Nobel Prize for her experiment disproving a physics law known as "conservation of parity."

1964 Cyrus Tang starts a steel warehouse business.

1968 Apollo 8 blasts off for a trip around the moon, propelled by a Saturn V rocket developed by Wernher von Braun and his team of engineers.

1969 Apollo 11 lands safely on the moon on July 20 using the geological plans of Farouk El-Baz.

1973 Henry Kissinger signs the Paris Accord, a peace treaty ending the Vietnam War.

1979 George Soros begins his philanthropy with financial assistance to after-school programs, regions struck by natural disaster, and causes that support justice, public health, and independent media.

1984 Madeleine May Kunin is elected the governor of Vermont.

1995 Pierre Omidyar starts eBay.

1996 President Bill Clinton nominates Madeleine Albright to become the first female secretary of state.

2001 Elaine Chao is the first Asian American woman appointed U.S. secretary of labor.

2003 Arnold Schwarzenegger becomes governor of California.

2004 Ave Kludze and his team of engineers design the EVA IR camera for space-walking astronauts.

2006 Anousheh Ansari becomes the first female private space explorer and the first astronaut of Iranian descent.

2009 Preet Bharara is appointed U.S. attorney for the Southern District of New York.

2012 Mazie Hirono is elected to the U.S. Senate, making her the first female Asian American senator.

2013 Yea Ji Sea joins the U.S. Army through the MAVNI program.

2015 Navy destroyer USS *Rafael Peralta* is dedicated in honor of Rafael Peralta's service and sacrifice to his country.

2016 Pramila Jayapal is elected to the U.S. House of Representatives.

Fang Wong joins the VA's Advisory Committee on Minority Veterans.

2017 Kashoua Kristy Yang is elected Milwaukee County circuit court judge, becoming the first female Hmong judge in the United States.

Maria Daume finishes basic training, becoming one of the first women to join the U.S. Marines infantry.

2018 Ilhan Omar becomes the first Somali American, first naturalized citizen from Africa, and second Muslim woman elected to the U.S. House of Representatives.

GLOSSARY

anti-Semitism (an-ti-SEM-i-ti-zem)—prejudice and discrimination against Jewish people because of their cultural background, religion, or race

authoritarianism (aw-thor-uh-TARE-ee-uhn-iz-uhm)—a form of government with strong central power and limited political freedoms

chief warrant officer 3 (CHEEF WOR-uhnt OF-uh-sur THREE)—a high-ranking commissioned officer in the U.S. armed forces

communism (KAHM-yuh-ni-zuhm)—a way of organizing a country so that all the land, houses, and factories belong to the government, and the profits are shared by all

indigenous (in-DIJ-uhn-uhs)—native to a place

infantry (IN-fuhn-tree)—soldiers trained to fight on foot

NATO (NAY-toe)—North Atlantic Treaty Organization; NATO includes countries from North America and Europe that have formed an alliance to help maintain peace and defend one another

nonpartisan (non-PAR-tuh-zuhn)—when something is not biased toward any particular political group

progressive (pruh-GRESS-iv)—in favor of improvement, progress, and reform, especially in political or social matters

revolution (rev-uh-LOO-shuhn)—an uprising by a group of people against a system of government or a way of life

think tank (THINGK TANGK)—an institute that performs research and advocacy about a particular topic, often in association with political parties

READ MORE

Imery-Garcia, Ash. *How Mexican Immigrants Made America Home.* New York: Rosen Central, 2018.

Perl, Lila and Erin L. McCoy. *Immigration: Welcome or Not?* New York: Cavendish Square Publishing, 2019.

Wallace, Sandra Neil and Rich Wallace. *First Generation: 36 Trailblazing Immigrants and Refugees Who Make America Great.* New York: Little, Brown and Company, 2018.

INTERNET SITES

Kids Discover: Immigration
https://online.kidsdiscover.com/unit/immigration

PBS American Experience: Immigration and Deportation at Ellis Island
http://www.pbs.org/wgbh/americanexperience/features/goldman-immigration-and-deportation-ellis-island/

Smithsonian National Museum of American History: Latino History
https://americanhistory.si.edu/topics/latino-history

SOURCE NOTES

Page 16, "I think everything . . ." James Clark, "She Was Born in a Russian Prison and Became a Trailblazing Infantry Marine," *Task and Purpose*, March 3, 2020, https://taskandpurpose.com/community/born-russian-prison-became-us-marine-infantry-next, Accessed June 21, 2020.

Page 21, "I believe success . . ." Teresa Watanabe, "He Gives to Stir Charity in Others," *Los Angeles Times*, June 15, 2008, https://www.latimes.com/archives/la-xpm-2008-jun-15-me-tang15-story.html, Accessed July 21, 2020.

Page 32, "This was the source . . ." Katherine Kleeman, "Madeleine May Kunin," *Jewish Women's Archive*, https://jwa.org/encyclopedia/article/kunin-madeleine, Accessed July 21, 2020.

Page 41, "For years, I had this . . ." Ella Nilsen, "Pramila Jayapal is Congress's Activist Insider," *Vox*, February 20, 2019, https://www.vox.com/2019/2/20/18141001/pramila-jayapal-congressional-progressive-caucus-house-democrats, Accessed July 21, 2020.

Page 53, "She and my father . . ." Secretary Elaine L. Chao, "Tributes to Ruth Mulan Chu Chao," September 20, 2007, https://www.elainelchao.com/speeches/view/tributes-to-ruth-mulan-chu-chao, Accessed July 21, 2020.

INDEX

IMMIGRANTS WHO DARED

Courage. Leadership. Vision. Inventiveness. Daring. That's what the immigrants to the United States profiled in this series have in common. They came to America to seek better lives for themselves and their families. And they benefited our nation in all kinds of ways, from serving in government and the military to building industries to inventing amazing products.

IMMIGRANTS WHO SERVED THE NATION

Some of the most important roles in American life have been filled by people born outside the United States. Immigrants have served in the military since the Civil War. Some immigrants have made fortunes and given them away—to create libraries, fund after-school programs, and protect citizens' civil rights. Still others have held political office or served our nation as ambassadors or—literally—rocket scientists. Here are 25 immigrants who have served our nation in these and other important ways.

TITLES IN THIS SERIES

$8.95 US / $11.95 CAN
ISBN 978-1-4966-9680-9

capstone
capstonepub.com

F&P Text Level Gradient™
Officially Leveled by Fountas & Pinnell

For leveling information, please visit
www.CapstoneClassroom.com